This Notebook belongs to

Legendary Notebook

NAME:

PHONE:

EMAIL:

January 2020

Sunday	Monday	Tuesday	Wednesday	Thursday	Friday	Saturday
29 Dec 2019	30	31	1 Jan 2020	2	3	4
5	6	7	8	9	10	11
12	13	14	15	16	17	18
19	20	21	22	23	24	25
26	27	28	29	30	31	1 Feb

February 2020

Sunday	Monday	Tuesday	Wednesday	Thursday	Friday	Saturday
26 Jan 2020	27	28	29	30	31	1 Feb
2	3	4	5	6	7	8
9	10	11	12	13	14	15
16	17	18	19	20	21	22
23	24	25	26	27	28	29

March 2020

Sunday	Monday	Tuesday	Wednesday	Thursday	Friday	Saturday
1 Mar 2020	2	3	4	5	6	7
8	9	10	11	12	13	14
15	16	17	18	19	20	21
22	23	24	25	26	27	28
29	30	31	1 Apr	2	3	4

April 2020

Sunday	Monday	Tuesday	Wednesday	Thursday	Friday	Saturday
29 Mar 2020	30	31	1 Apr	2	3	4
5	6	7	8	9	10	11
12	13	14	15	16	17	18
19	20	21	22	23	24	25
26	27	28	29	30	1 May	2

May 2020

Sunday	Monday	Tuesday	Wednesday	Thursday	Friday	Saturday
26 Apr 2020	27	28	29	30	1 May	2
3	4	5	6	7	8	9
10	11	12	13	14	15	16
17	18	19	20	21	22	23
24	25	26	27	28	29	30
31	1 Jun	2	3	4	5	6

June 2020

Sunday	Monday	Tuesday	Wednesday	Thursday	Friday	Saturday
31 May 2020	1 Jun	2	3	4	5	6
7	8	9	10	11	12	13
14	15	16	17	18	19	20
21	22	23	24	25	26	27
28	29	30	1 Jul	2	3	4

July 2020

Sunday	Monday	Tuesday	Wednesday	Thursday	Friday	Saturday
28 Jun 2020	29	30	1 Jul	2	3	4
5	6	7	8	9	10	11
12	13	14	15	16	17	18
19	20	21	22	23	24	25
26	27	28	29	30	31	1 Aug

August 2020

Sunday	Monday	Tuesday	Wednesday	Thursday	Friday	Saturday
26 Jul 2020	27	28	29	30	31	1 Aug
2	3	4	5	6	7	8
9	10	11	12	13	14	15
16	17	18	19	20	21	22
23	24	25	26	27	28	29
30	31	1 Sep	2	3	4	5

September 2020

Sunday	Monday	Tuesday	Wednesday	Thursday	Friday	Saturday
30 Aug 2020	31	1 Sep	2	3	4	5
6	7	8	9	10	11	12
13	14	15	16	17	18	19
20	21	22	23	24	25	26
27	28	29	30	1 Oct	2	3

October 2020

Sunday	Monday	Tuesday	Wednesday	Thursday	Friday	Saturday
27 Sep 2020	28	29	30	1 Oct	2	3
4	5	6	7	8	9	10
11	12	13	14	15	16	17
18	19	20	21	22	23	24
25	26	27	28	29	30	31

November 2020

Sunday	Monday	Tuesday	Wednesday	Thursday	Friday	Saturday
1 Nov 2020	2	3	4	5	6	7
8	9	10	11	12	13	14
15	16	17	18	19	20	21
22	23	24	25	26	27	28
29	30	1 Dec	2	3	4	5

December 2020

Sunday	Monday	Tuesday	Wednesday	Thursday	Friday	Saturday
29 Nov 2020	30	1 Dec	2	3	4	5
6	7	8	9	10	11	12
13	14	15	16	17	18	19
20	21	22	23	24	25	26
27	28	29	30	31	1 Jan 2021	2

Made in the USA
Monee, IL
22 June 2021